This book belongs to

....

....

Nita Mehta
PUBLICATIONS

Tales of
GANESH

© Copyright 2005 *Nita Mehta* PUBLICATIONS

WORLD RIGHTS RESERVED: The contents—all text and illustrations are original and copyrighted. No portion of this book shall be reproduced, stored in a retrieval system or transmitted by any means, electronic, mechanical, photocopying, recording or otherwise, without the written permission of the publishers.

While every precaution is taken in the preparation of this book, the publisher and the author assume no responsibility for errors or omissions. Neither is any liability assumed for damages resulting from the use of information contained herein.

TRADEMARKS ACKNOWLEDGED: Trademarks used, if any, are acknowledged as trademarks of their respective owners. These are used as reference only and no trademark infringement is intended upon.

First Edition 2005

ISBN 81-7676-045-5

Illustrations: *Nita Mehta* PUBLICATIONS
  Artist : Rajesh Prajapati

Layout and laser typesetting:

National Information Technology Academy
3A/3, Asaf Ali Road
New Delhi-110002
☎ 23252948

Published by:

3A/3 Asaf Ali Road, New Delhi-110002
Tel: 91-11-23250091, 29214011, 23252948, 29218727
Fax: 91-11-29225218, 91-11-23250091
E-Mail : nitamehta@email.com, snab@snabindia.com
Website : http://www.nitamehta.com, http://www.snabindia.com

Contributing Writers:
Subhash Mehta
Tanya Mehta

Editorial & Proofreading:
Ekta
Deepali

Distributed by :
THE VARIETY BOOK DEPOT
A.V.G. Bhavan, M 3 Con Circus,
New Delhi - 110 001
Tel : 23417175, 23412567; Fax : 23415335
Email: varietybookdepot@rediffmail.com

Printed by :
AJANTA OFFSET & PACKAGING LTD

Tales of
GANESH

ANURAG MEHTA

VANEETA VAID

Who is Ganesh?

Ganesh is the elephant headed Hindu God. He is the son of **Lord Shiv** and **Goddess Parvati**. Ganesh is the lord of wisdom and good will. He is much revered by Hindus. There are 108 names of veneration for lord Ganesh!

Ganesh even has his own vehicle to ride. Do you know what? A rat! Thus, it is said that Ganesh has the extreme strength of an elephant to bulldoze his way on the surface and also the intricate agility of a rat to burrow and manoeuvre under surface!

Where does Ganesh live? He lives in the heavenly abode called *Kailash*. Does Ganesh have any brother or sister? Yes. After the birth of Ganesh, one more son was born to Lord Shiv & Parvati. He was called **Kartikeya**.

Shiv and Parvati, like any other parents, had their hands full in bringing up Ganesh! Ganesh was an adorable cherub with all the naughtiness of a young boy. However, sometimes his profound wisdom surprised every one, including his parents.

How Ganesh Got his Elephant Head?

"I need to go for a bath! But I am alone and there is no one to guard my home!" fretted Goddess Parvati to herself. Why was the Goddess alone? Well, her husband Lord Shiv was away fighting wars with the demons. Parvati thought for some time and then said, "I will create my own guard." She rubbed her body with jasmine oil and sandal paste. Then, she scraped off some of the scented paste from her body. She mixed the scented paste with water and clay from the river *Ganga* and made a clay boy from it. Holding the clay child close to her lips, Parvati infused life into him. And lo behold! The clay child became a handsome young boy.

"You are our son from now on!" Parvati proudly told the boy. "Guard my home whilst I bathe! Do not allow any one to intrude or enter the hut!" she instructed the boy. Then she went in for a bath. The boy stood in strict vigil. Unexpectedly, Lord Shiv returned home.

"Who are you?" Shiv questioned the boy who was not allowing him to enter his own home! "Who are you?" countered the boy!

Now, Lord Shiv, master of the universe and manifestation of the supreme almighty of the worlds, was not at all pleased! He bristled and frowned demanding to be allowed to enter his home. However, the boy persistently refused to let Shiv enter! Shiv became very angry and a clash ensued. The fall out was that Shiv chopped the boy's head off! When Parvati came out of her bath, she was horrified to see what had happened! Cursing Shiv, she wept uncontrollably. Shiv too was stricken with shock and grief. Unwittingly, he had killed his own son! He had to do something to comfort his grieving spouse! So, he turned to his soldiers and ordered, "Go into the forest! Bring the head of the first living being you see sleeping, facing the north!"

"Why north?" wondered the soldiers.

"The northward journey means a journey towards illumination to the path of Gods. Moreover, we all know that the direction north is a beneficial one!" explained Lord Shiv.

The soldiers immediately followed his command. Soon, they came across an elephant who was sleeping, facing the north. The soldiers cut its head off and gave it to Shiv. Shiv immediately placed the head on the life less boy's severed neck. With his new elephant head, the boy came alive. "We will name our son Ganesh!" said Shiv.

"I declare that Ganesh shall be regarded by one and all, as the remover of obstacles and he should be offered worship first, before any form of worship is offered to any other Gods!" Shiv furthermore announced. Ganesh was also made the leader of Shiv's *ganas* (assistants) and thus became **Ganpati**. Parvati was overjoyed. It did not matter to her that her son now had an elephant head. He was well and alive and that's all she wanted.

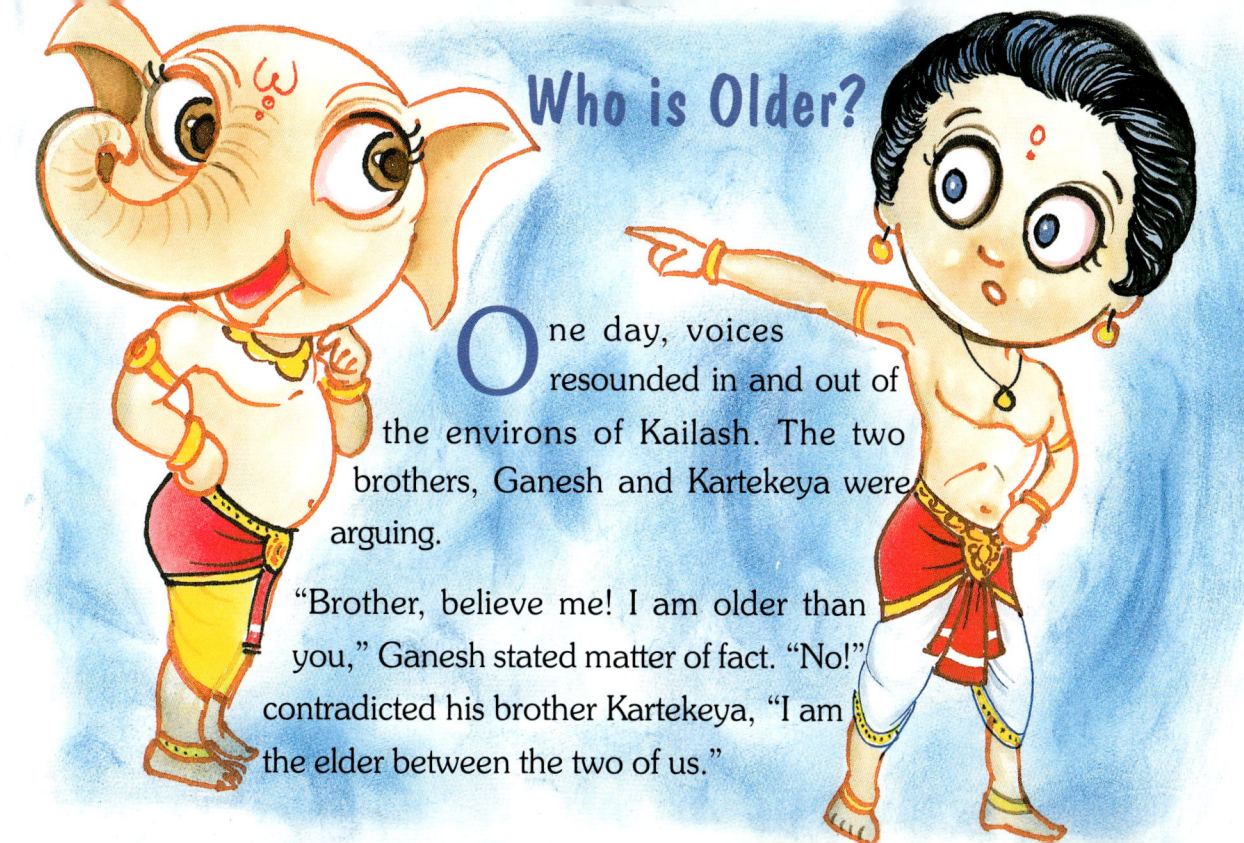

Who is Older?

One day, voices resounded in and out of the environs of Kailash. The two brothers, Ganesh and Kartekeya were arguing.

"Brother, believe me! I am older than you," Ganesh stated matter of fact. "No!" contradicted his brother Kartekeya, "I am the elder between the two of us."

Why were the two brothers quarrelling? Actually, it all started when the Gods of heaven presented Shiv and Parvati with a rare fruit. Now the brothers verbally tangled over who should get the fruit.

"The elder one should," mused their parents! Sigh! And that's how a strife between the brothers ensued! Soon, the dispute heated up and finally their parents had to intervene. "Father, tell him that I am the elder of the two! I should get the fruit," blurted Ganesh, his trunk curling and whirling agitatedly.

Kartekeya shrugged saying, "Father, Mother! Convince Ganesh that I am the elder!"

"This is getting quite serious," Shiv whispered to his wife.

"Yes! The brothers are getting into a terrible quarrel, sire! Do something!" Parvati urged.

"Very well!" Shiv pondered and then spoke, "Sons, we will resolve your argument with a solution. Here is the solution: whoever can tour the whole world and come back first to this starting point, will be given the right to be the elder brother and get the fruit!"

"Here I go," declared Kartekeya! Before anything, he flew off at once on his vehicle, the peacock, to make a circuit of the world! But Ganesh did not move. His vehicle, the rat, was raring to go, but Ganesh just sat on it!

Did Ganesh move eventually? Did he begin the race? Well, yes he did! He moved, not to dash around the world, but only to circle his parents! His parents were surprised.

Why was Ganesh still here? How would he cross continents, mountains, rivers and lakes if he did not leave?

Ganesh just kept circling his parents with not a care in the world! His parents stared at him, feeling very confused.

In a while, Ganesh came up to his parents and said, "Divine parents, I have circled the world so many times. Give me the fruit and declare me first!"

"Ganesh, we cannot do that! You did not circle the world with its seas, mountains and continents. You just hovered and circled around us," admonished his parents gently.

"But I have circled the world and come first father," Ganesh insisted. "What?" uttered the two puzzled parents. Ganesh bowed in front of Shiv and Parvati and said solemnly, "You two are the world!

My heavenly parents represent the entire manifested universe!" Hearing this, Shiv and Parvati broke into a cheer and proudly acknowledged that for a boy so young, Ganesh was really very wise. When Kartekeya returned, he was told of what Ganesh had said. He too had to agree that Ganesh had shown very mature wisdom. Thus, Ganesh was declared the elder of the two and given the precious fruit.

The Moon Teases Ganesh!

"Aha, today is my birthday and I shall eat lots of *laddoos*," Ganesh slurped to his rat. "Let's go! A devotee has invited me to his house for a feast!"

Ganesh was extremely happy when he saw the pile of *laddoos* set before him at the devotee's home!

"Munch-yum-munch-munch!" Ganesh eagerly picked off the *laddoos* with his trunk from the plate. He ate and ate till his belly began to swell. "Burp!" went Ganesh and his belly shook!

"Now, I am satisfied! I have eaten so many *laddoos* that I can hardly move! Rat, take me home." He mounted his rat and left.

The rat with Ganesh on his back weaved through paths. Suddenly, a snake abruptly came in their way! The rat skidded and in doing so, he threw Ganesh off!

Bump! Ganesh rolled and with a thump, his stomach burst open!

Plonk-plonk-plonk! *Laddoos* spilled from his tummy! Horrified Ganesh looked around, his trunk curling with acute embarrassment! He was sure that no one was around to see his ridiculous situation!

"Wait, rat! Let me put the *laddoos* back into my stomach," Ganesh uttered. He quickly filled his stomach again but realized that the *laddoos* kept spilling out from his open belly.

"Aha! I have an idea," Ganesh muttered, glancing at the slinking snake! Whup! He seized the snake.

"Sorry snake, I am going to use you as a belt to hold my tummy full of *laddoos*."

Saying so, Ganesh did just that. He tightened the 'snake belt' and held back all the *laddoos* into his big belly!

"Let's go," Ganesh instructed his ride. Just as Ganesh remounted his vehicle, he heard a chuckle.

"Who is that?" Ganesh curiously flapped his ears and looked about. There was no one on the surface.

"Ha-ha-ha, so funny, ha-ha! Using a snake belt to stop *laddoos* from spilling," again someone giggled.

Now, Ganesh was good and proper angry. Who was mocking at him? He looked up and saw the culprit. It was the moon. The moon was giggling helplessly at the sight of Ganesh and his stomach full of *laddoos* tied with a snake!

Ganesh went crimson with anger. "How dare you laugh at me," shouted Ganesh at the moon. But the moon was quite taken in by the funny sight and kept up his smirk.

This further angered Ganesh and he broke a part of his tusk and hurled it at the moon, saying piercingly, "I curse you! You will never shine at night now!"

Till then, the moon used to shine every night. Just as soon as Ganesh said that, the moon disappeared and the sky went inky black. Ganesh rode off fuming.

"Aieeee!!! Where is the moon?" the people on earth frantically asked. "Where is the moon?" said the Gods in heaven too! Nights became miserable for the earth and heaven inmates. Gloomy darkness besieged them every evening. "This is Ganesh's doing. He is angry with the moon for laughing at him! Let's go and beg Ganesh to forgive the moon!" suggested someone.

So people, as well as the Gods went to Ganesh and pleaded, "Please bring the moon back! Please forgive it for laughing at you!"

Now, Ganesh was not the one to carry grudges. "Hmmm, I will bring the moon back," said Ganesh. Everyone clapped happily at this. "But, on one condition," declared Ganesh, still a little miffed at the moon's audacity.

"What condition?" queried all.

"Henceforth, the moon is sentenced to wax and wane! It will alternate between a shining fortnight and a dark fortnight. Each period will end by a full moon and a new moon."

"Oh, thank you!" everyone bowed. A waxing and waning moon was better than no moon, you see!

Did you know that till today people consider it inauspicious to look at the moon on Ganesh Chaturthi! Ganesh Chaturthi is celebrated as Ganesh's birthday and on this day people do not look at the moon as it dared to laugh at Ganesh!

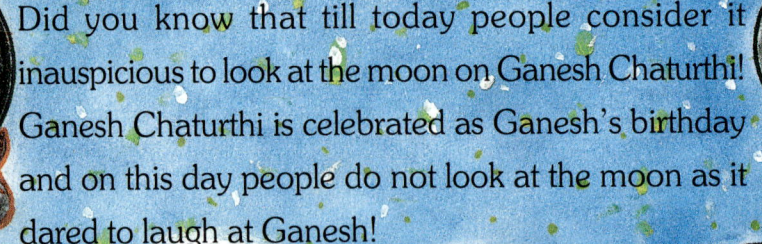

Ganpati and the God of Wealth

"I am truly very rich!"

"I really have a lot of riches," bragged Kuber, the treasurer of the heavens, vainly to himself. "I think I shall go to Kailash and invite Lord Shiv and his spouse Goddess Parvati for a meal! They will come to my celestial kingdom of Alkapuri and see for themselves how wealthy I am!" Deciding this, Kuber presented himself in front of Shiv.

"Thank you so much Kuber, for your kind invite for lunch," answered Shiv when Kuber requested him to come for lunch. "But I am afraid, I will have to refuse. Parvati and I have pressing engagements elsewhere." Shiv knew quite well why he was being invited. Kuber had always been a silly show-off. Kuber was unable to hide his disappointment, so Shiv quickly added, "I suggest you take Ganesh with you for lunch!"

Ganesh nodded his head happily. He loved food and a lunch invitation promised a great deal of good eats!

Kuber, of course, kept boasting about his glory and his own riches as Ganesh accompanied him back to Alkapuri. Finally, Kuber and Ganesh reached Alkapuri.

Soon, Ganesh was greeted by a traditional perfumed bath for an extravagant welcome at the palace entrance. After that, they entered into the obviously luxurious palace. Kuber proudly strutted along the ornate corridors hoping Ganesh was noticing his prosperity!

Ganesh was led to an even more ostentatious dining area. Servants carrying trays laden with food lined the hall. Apparently overjoyed, Ganesh sat down to eat. His appetite was ravenous. He finished off all that was served to him.

"Bring me more food! Bring me all the cooked food in the kitchen!" Hurriedly, the palace servants ran up and down serving Ganesh who seemed to be very hungry! The servants huffed, puffed and panted piling food into Ganesh's plate. Ganesh ate and ate and ate. Dishes emptied faster than they could be filled.

"I am still hungry," Ganesh said petulantly. "I want more food."

"The food is finished, sire," the head cook whispered to Kuber.

Ganesh heard that and bellowed, "What? Food is finished! But I am still hungry," Ganesh grabbed his plate and munched it up. The servants as well as Kuber shrank. Ganesh ran to the kitchen and began to eat the empty vessels too! Then, he went to Kuber's treasury and began eating the pearls and gold and gems. Kuber saw his boundless treasure dwindling before his eyes until all that remained were a couple of pearls in the corner. Kuber could have cried in anguish. His treasury had never stood empty! Still, Ganesh was not satisfied.

Ganesh went on eating everything that came his way! Gasp! Even the furniture of the palace, the gardens, the trees, everything! He began to eat through the city of Alkapuri too!

Kuber watched horrified. He stood with folded hands and appealed to Ganesh not to destroy his city.

"I am still hungry," said Ganesh. Then, Kuber noticed the little God looking at him with a wicked gleam in his eyes. "Since there is nothing left to eat, I think I'll eat you!"

Kuber fled with the little God close behind. He ran to Shiv and fell at his feet, quivering with fear.

"Help! My almighty lord, help! Ganesh is eating everything! His hunger is insatiable! He is threatening to eat me too!" Shiv smiled and said, "Kuber, take this roasted rice and feed Ganesh." Kuber bowed humbly and served Ganesh. Ganesh ate the roasted rice and suddenly he was not hungry any more. "I am full now," sighed Ganesh.

Kuber heaved a sigh of relief. He saw Ganesh and Shiv smiling at each other and realized he had been guilty of pride and vanity. "Forgive me, lord, for my pride in my wealth. I had forgotten that it is you who gave it to me." Thus, saying so, Kuber left.

Later Kuber thought to himself, "Lord Ganesh taught me a good lesson. By demanding more food, he was showing me that even the best of cuisine brought to him with an intention to show off, brings no satisfaction. Yet, just a handful of ordinary roasted rice given with love and devotion gave him so much of contentment and he was happy! I expressed my love and devotion to God by material opulence and not by genuine feelings!!"

Ganesh Writes the Mahabharat

Sage Ved Vyasa conceived a beautiful poem in his mind. He called it the *Mahabharat*. Ved Vyasa wanted to tell the whole world about his poem. Somehow, he did not know how to do so. He decided to meditate and ask the creator of the world, Lord Brahma, to suggest a way.

"Write the verses of this eloquent poem. Make a chronicle for future generations to read!" Lord Brahma instructed sage Ved Vyasa.

"As you command, my lord," Ved Vyasa bowed. He, however, added with folded hands, "Lord Brahma, I would like to request you to assign me an assistant."

"Ask Ganesh, the son of Shiv and Parvati," suggested Brahma.

"Will you be my assistant whilst I write the epic of Mahabharat?" the sage asked Ganesh.

"Of course!" Ganesh nodded readily. "What do I have to do?"

"Well, I shall dictate verses and you shall write them down," answered the sage.

"No problem!" Ganesh said.

Lord Ganesh agreed but he had conditions too. Ganesh said to the sage, "I will do so. But if you halt or hesitate in speaking, I will stop writing and your epic will never be written."

"I agree, but you must also fully comprehend the meaning of the poems as you write and not just blindly write them as I say," answered Vyasa.

The elephant headed God gave his consent and they started writing the great epic, Mahabharat. We have read that Ganesh broke off his tusk to hurl it at the moon. But other legends claim that he broke his tusk at this time and used it as a pen to write Ved Vyasa's verses!

Ved Vyasa began his narration and Ganesh wrote it down fast. In fact, he was so fast that he did not give Ved Vyasa enough time to even catch his breath!

Ganesh unmindful of this, went on writing at super speed. Poor Ved Vyasa began to go blue in the face, but Ganesh scribbled on rapidly!

"I will die, if I do not take a break and catch my breath," thought a panicky Ved Vyasa. "I must think of something."

Ved Vyasa suddenly lapsed to create a very complicated and tricky stanza for the verses. For a split second, Ganesh was confused and he paused to understand before writing.

"Whooooooooosh!" In those fractions of time, Ved Vyasa inhaled gulps of air!

And so, whenever Ved Vyasa needed a break, he would narrate a difficult phrase. In a flash, Ganesh would stall to understand the verse and swiftly Ved Vyasa gasped in a breath!

Thus, the original Mahabharat contains many difficult stanzas placed at intervals throughout the length of the epic.

By writing the verses of the great poem Mahabharat, Lord Ganesh became the first stenographer in the world! He had taken down the largest book ever composed, dictated by sage Vyasa.